I CARE
TO SHARE:

I CARE TO SHARE:

A Manual for the Loving Care of _____

Dr. Debi Stewart

Cover Illustration by
Hilbert Bermejo

Library of Congress Control Number:		2011919034
ISBN:	Hardcover	978-1-4653-8648-9
	Softcover	978-1-4653-8647-2
	Ebook	978-1-4653-8649-6

This book was printed in the United States of America.

To order additional copies of this book, contact:
Xlibris Corporation
1-888-795-4274
www.Xlibris.com
Orders@Xlibris.com
103701

CONTENTS

DEDICATION

THIS BOOK IS dedicated to the loving memory of my father, Hugh Taney, and in loving honor of my mother, Arlene Taney. Dad was always doing for others, whether it was family, neighbors, coworkers, or friends. He was the first to call whenever there was a problem, and he would respond immediately and work tirelessly until the situation was resolved. In 1999, our world changed, as Dad had a stroke that resulted in him being dependent for the first time.

My mother, Arlene Taney, dedicated the next five years to the tough mental and physical challenge of providing the loving care Dad required day and night, committed to keeping him in the house he built and as active as he and she were capable of achieving. During the five years, they celebrated their sixtieth anniversary, although we are not certain that Dad really understood. In July of 2004, Dad required St. Luke's Hospice services as his condition deteriorated rapidly and his care was more than Mom could provide. He passed on July 12, 2004, at home.

Extreme gratitude goes out to St. Luke's Hospice, with one dollar of each book sale being donated to their (St. Luke's Hospice) continued ability to provide high quality personalized care to those, like my father, who wish to remain at home in their final stage of life.

ACKNOWLEDGMENTS

S PECIAL THANKS TO my husband, Gary Stewart, who always listens and encourages me whenever I have a new idea or venture. Sincere appreciation goes to my son, Cory McClanahan, for his love shown in the time and energy he gave as a sounding board and advisor while I worked through the extended process of developing this book. I hope my life-long learning and achievement serves as a role model to my son and my niece, Brooke Shupe, and nephew, Brent Taney, who I love like my own children. My brother, Dr. Gary Taney, deserves special thanks for the love and support he has shown for me throughout my lifetime.

Many friends offered support for the cause and encouragement along the way that I wish to thank Ellen and Donnie Weeks, Doug Perry, Ginny Boyd, Julie Ausmus, Ken Tongue, Sherri Shatto, Tammy Becker, Debra Slaughter, Sue Woods, Judy Hankins, Sandra Thompson, and my sixth grade gifted class at South Valley Middle School in Liberty, Missouri—they are the bright light in my mornings!

A special friend who encouraged me to complete the book and assisted me with the wheelchair section, Edwin Pepper, Sr. (residing in the Gower Missouri Nursing Home) will always have a special place in my heart.

Finally, I am grateful to Xlibris Publishing for providing such great support throughout the process of finalizing the manuscript to publishing and marketing. This was a very thorough process that was greatly needed by me, as a first-time author.

PREFACE

T HE IDEA OF creating this manual came when my mother (Dad's caregiver) desired to travel with her sisters for a week to Arizona to attend a family wedding. Mom asked my brother (a physician) and me (a nurse and teacher) to share the care of Dad by splitting up the week. Many weeks prior to leaving, Mom called several times to provide details of Dad's care as they occurred to her. Details such as "Tell your dad to take out his teeth bridge and be sure to hide it in the cabinet so he does not flush it down the toilet" . . . "Dad likes to drink out of the plastic cup" . . . "Dad will get upset if his feet are covered at night", etc. I knew I would not remember all these details coming to me at all different times unless they were written down. I also knew my mom would not enjoy the much deserved time off if I did not take each worry seriously. I developed this loving care manual as a result. I spent time with mom filling it out, and I know when she traveled she felt more at peace. She provided all the details needed, and we cared enough to have it recorded. It is obvious that my brother and I had the medical knowledge to care for Dad; however, we did not have the detail routines and preference knowledge to prevent his easily induced impatience (result of his stroke). Dad's routine did not change very much, and as a result, it was an enjoyable week spent with him.

This book was written for those who provide care for a dependent loved one, whether the loved one is an elderly family member or a young disabled child. The purpose of the book is to assist the caregiver to document the details of the daily care and assistance provided. With this documentation, it is hoped that there will be peace of mind for the caregiver in the event that someone else would need to take over the care. The peace of mind that they have done everything they could to facilitate their loved one having continuity of care consistent with the high level currently being given. Many children and adults that require care also expect and rely on the routine of that care—their emotional and physical safety can be impacted by even minor changes.

With this book, the prompts assist in covering the routines, safe movement, and care. Whether the substitute caregiver is highly trained, family, or friend, this care manual can be used as a guide to keep the consistency or as a problem solving manual when problems or resistance arises.

In the event that the loved one is hospitalized or enters into a long-term care facility, the book can accompany him/her. With the patient load that these facilities have, it is unlikely that the book will be read cover to cover by the many professionals sharing the care. However, if there is an issue or resistance that presents great problems, the manual may offer the information to get over that hurdle and be quite a valuable resource.

Now that Dad has passed on, the manual that Mom and I filled out serves as a tribute to the love that she showed to Dad for the care given. Dad's hard labor and sacrifices for his family were very apparent over the years. This book opened my eyes to the sacrifices Mom made 24/7 for Dad and the great love they had for each other.

INTRODUCTION

I CARE TO Share: A Manual For the Loving Care of . . . contains prompts and lines for individualized responses. Recognizing that the care that is being given can come automatically and not be in the forefront of the caregiver's mind, the prompts are designed to stimulate the caregiver to think through and record task steps. The manual covers usual events in the course of a day. This provides the best possible chance that the daily care can be replicated by someone else in the event that the caregiver is no longer able or available to provide the care, short or long term.

The manual is written in sections which allows the caregiver to provide basic information regarding emergency information, medications, important people, hour-by-hour typical day, meal preferences and instructions for preparation, managing meals, grooming and hygiene, bathing/showering and toileting, ambulating, wheelchair, changing positions, bedtime routine, recreation/entertainment, church/community, restaurant and eating out, and a short biography.

A short biographical section provides information that a substitute caregiver can use for conversation starters. This is extremely important if there is a shift from family to professional caregivers that the loved one may not know. If the loved one is unable to speak or carry on a conversation, the information in this section is still quite valuable. It enables the new caregiver to use familiar terms, thus providing some comfort in bridging the gap of being a stranger.

Lastly there is an appendix section with additional resources that may be helpful. This book represents a passion of mine to assist both the loved one and the caregiver to have the most peace of mind and quality of life possible. While I have a strong nursing background and experience in convalescent care, I cannot write a manual that will contain prompts to address every person's needs. Therefore, some generic blank checklists are included in the Appendix that can be filled in showing step-by-step procedures for complicated treatments. For this section, I highly encourage the caregiver to write a draft of the checklist and consult with the loved one's doctor, nurse, or home health professional to make sure the checklist is specific enough and accurate. In some cases, there may be written instructions from these professionals that can be glued or taped to one of the blank pages and referenced in the appropriate section of the manual. This loving care manual is a living document that can be modified as conditions change.

The manual is intended to be written in, notes made in the margins or in the back, and updated as needed. If the manual becomes too full and there have been many changes in the loved one's condition and care required, it may be necessary to purchase a new blank book for clarity. The price of the book has been kept as low as possible, so this can be an affordable option.

I strongly encourage each caregiver and family of the caregiver to read the section entitled "How to Use this Manual." There are many great ideas that lead to quality entries and enrich family relationships.

HOW TO USE THIS MANUAL

THE PURPOSE OF this "Manual for the Loving Care" is to benefit both the caregiver and the loved one receiving the care. In order for the manual to achieve the maximum benefit to both, some tips for the creation and use of the manual are included in this chapter. Based on personal experience of assisting my mother to complete the manual and then as a substitute caregiver using that manual, I can offer several suggestions. The core suggestions are in italics, with further explanation in regular font. These are by no means all inclusive. If anyone has further ideas, I am very interested in receiving them.

First, the manual is a great gift; *a gift of love for the caregiver and the one receiving care.* Caregivers are often very busy, and in order to keep this manual from being one more thing to get done, *plan times to assist with its completion.* This also serves many purposes. Quality time is spent with the caregiver, and it *provides a great medium for the recognition of the vast amount of responsibility, work, and love that goes into the daily care being provided.* Giving the book as a gift is a great first step; spending time to give value to the details of the loving care being provided is the second and equally as important aspect of the gift.

The manual is divided into sections for ease of completion. Since attention to detail is very important, it is suggested that *completion be done in more than one sitting and with assistance from at least one other person* close to the caregiver. Tasks are always more pleasant when done with assistance and companionship. Once the completion is divided into sessions, the caregiver should *preview the upcoming section prior to planning to fill it in.* Then for the next few days, pay special attention to the details of care that is covered in the section soon to be completed. When the time comes to complete that section, it will be easier to put the care into words. If it would be helpful, *a small tape recorder can be used set nearby for the caregiver to narrate the steps of some more complicated tasks as they are actually being performed.* Then the dictation can be played back and transposed into the manual.

I encourage the caregiver to fill in as many sections of the manual as possible, even if the person receiving care is able to speak for him/herself. When a change in routine occurs, sometimes those that were able to communicate with their family find it difficult to communicate to someone new. Frustration can impair their mental thinking and communication ability. The more that is included in this book, the better the chance to reduce that frustration and keep the continuity intact.

Place reminders on the calendar to verify the continued accuracy and update the manual. When placing doctor appointments on the calendar, add a reminder to update the "loving care manual" for the day following the appointment. If the loved one is hospitalized, take the manual with you (it is purposefully a small size to fit into a suitcase or purse). *Update it while medical, occupation therapists, social workers, rehabilitation, and home health professionals are available and preparing for discharge, including the instructions for new medications.* This way the entries can be reviewed with these professionals for accuracy and clarity. *Recording the entries will assist in better understanding of changes in care,* as writing information down assists in comprehension and retention.

If the occasion occurs that the care is relinquished, short or long term, and hiring of outside care is necessary, it is suggested that this *loving care manual be required reading* for the hired caregiver(s). This serves two purposes: it assists in maintaining continuity of care which is best for the loved one, and it emphasizes the high quality of care that is expected.

Use the blank pages in the Appendix of the book to include pictures that will illustrate any procedure that is difficult to clearly state in writing. Be sure to enter the written directions as clearly as possible with a notation to see the picture on whichever page it is attached. The old saying, "a picture is worth a thousand words," can be actualized in the back section.

Attach manufacturers' printed directions for equipment usage, troubleshooting and phone numbers for repair on these blank pages or notate the location of such documents on these pages. Some equipment needed for breathing, suctioning, etc., is vital to function properly and will require timely repair or replacement if malfunctions occur. This may be very important information that is overlooked if not included in the manual.

In nursing school, it is emphasized that hearing is the last sense to go and the first sense to return when a patient is under anesthetics. This is an important concept to keep in mind, as the loved one may be medicated to the extent that his/her communication is impaired or thought processes are delayed to the point that comprehension *appears* to be totally lacking. It is important to understand that the inability to follow directions or communicate effectively does not necessarily mean the individual does not understand what is being said. The section entitled "Communication" and the "Background Information" section should be completed thoroughly by the caregiver. These two sections are designed to provide resources for a new caregiver to initiate and encourage supportive dialogue, whether it is one-way or two-way communication.

SECTION 1

Emergency Information

Legal Name: _____

Address: _____

City: _____

State: _____ **Zip:** _____

Telephone Number: _____

Allergies: _____

_____

Primary Physician
Name: _____
Phone: _____

Specialists
Name: _____
Phone: _____

Name: _____
Phone: _____

Name: _____
Phone: _____

Ambulance Service:
Name: _____
Phone: _____

Hospital Preference
Name: _____

Emergency Contacts
Name: _____
Relationship: _____
Phone: Home _____
       Cell _____

Name: _____
Relationship: _____
Phone: Home _____
       Cell _____

Insurance/Medicaid/Medicare
Location of Cards:_____

_____

_____

Power of Attorney for Health Care
Document location: _____

_____

Advance Directive
Document Location:_____

_____

SECTION 2

Medications

Medication/Purpose	Dosage	Frequency	Time	Special Instructions

Medications

Medication/Purpose	Dosage	Frequency	Time	Special Instructions

Medications

Medication/Purpose	Dosage	Frequency	Time	Special Instructions

SECTION 3

Important People
Family/Friends

Spouse/Parent
Name: _____
Address: (If Different): _____

_____

Phone: Home _____
      Cell _____

Children
Name: _____
Address: _____

_____

Phone: Home _____
      Cell _____

Name: _____
Address: _____

_____

Phone: Home _____
      Cell _____

Name: _____
Address: _____
_____

Phone: Home _____
       Cell _____

Name: _____
Address: _____
_____

Phone: Home _____
       Cell _____

Sibling(s)
Name: _____
Address: _____
_____

Phone: Home _____
       Cell _____

Name: _____
Address: _____
_____

Phone: Home _____
       Cell _____

Name: _____

Address: _____

_____

Phone: Home _____

Cell _____

Name: _____

Address: _____

_____

Phone: Home _____

Cell _____

Neighbor(s)

Name: _____

Address: _____

_____

Phone: Home _____

Cell _____

Name: _____

Address: _____

_____

Phone: Home _____

Cell _____

Other Significant People

Name: _____

Address: _____

_____

Phone: Home _____

Cell _____

Name: _____

Address: _____

_____

Phone: Home _____

Cell _____

Name: _____

Address: _____

_____

Phone: Home _____

Cell _____

Name: _____

Address: _____

_____

Phone: Home _____

Cell _____

DR. DEBI STEWART

SECTION 4

Typical Day

Time	Activity
6:00 a.m.	
7:00 a.m.	
8:00 a.m.	
9:00 a.m.	
10:00 a.m.	

11:00 a.m.	
12:00 Noon	
1:00 p.m.	
2:00 p.m.	
3:00 p.m.	
4:00 p.m.	

DR. DEBI STEWART

5:00 p.m.	
6:00 p.m.	
7:00 p.m.	
8:00 p.m.	
9:00 p.m.	
10:00 p.m.	

11:00 p.m.	
12:00 a.m.	
1:00 a.m.	
2:00 a.m.	
3:00 a.m.	
4:00 a.m.	
5:00 a.m.	

DR. DEBI STEWART

SECTION 5

Meals

Breakfast

Food Preferences	Special Instructions for Preparation or Serving

Mid-morning Snack

Food Preferences	Special Instructions for Preparation or Serving

Lunch

Food Preferences	Special Instructions for Preparation or Serving

Afternoon Snack

Food Preferences	Special Instructions for Preparation or Serving

Dinner

Food Preferences	Special Instructions for Preparation or Serving

Evening Snack

Food Preferences	Special Instructions for Preparation or Serving

Other

Food Preferences	Special Instructions for Preparation or Serving

Managing Meals

Food Allergies: _____
_____

Food to Avoid: _____

Special Diet: _____
_____

Equipment Needed (Measuring,
caloric count, exchanges): _____
_____
_____

Food Dislikes: _____
_____

Special Instructions

Where Eats Meals: _____
_____

Feeding Instructions if Applicable:

_____
_____

Special Utensils: _____

_____

_____

_____

Other Needs (Extra time, reminders, bibs, pureeing or blending): _____

_____

_____

_____

_____

Fluid Intake (Encourage, limit, or restrict): _____

_____

_____

_____

_____

SECTION 6

Grooming/Hygiene

Oral Care

Denture: _____
Denture Cup Location: _____
_____

Gums/Lips: _____
_____

Natural Teeth
Toothbrush Location: _____
_____
Assistance Needed: _____
_____

Shaving
Frequency: _____
Time of Day or Night: _____
Type of Razor: _____
Location of Razor: _____
_____
Assistance Needed: _____

Nails and Foot Care

Special Instructions: _____

_____

_____

Precautions (Diabetes, Sores, Soaking
Nails, Ingrown Nails): _____

_____

_____

_____

**Lotion, Powder, Special Boots, Range of
Motion, Foot Board, etc.:** _____

_____

Circulation checks (Note procedure used and the
usual or normal): _____

_____

**Swelling
Ankle Measurement Range:** _____

_____

Coloration: _____

_____

Pedal Pulse Present (Feel on top of Foot): _____

_____

Temperature (Warm to touch, hot, cool): _____

_____

Bathing/Showering

Location: _____

_____

_____

Soaps:

_____

_____

Deodorant:

_____

_____

Lotion/Powder: _____

_____

Perfume/Cologne: _____

_____

Other: _____

_____

_____

_____

_____

Assistance Needed
Instructions of Entering and Exiting Tub or Shower: _____

_____

_____

_____

Bathing Assistance: _____

_____

_____

Drying Assistance: _____

_____

_____

Dressing

Type of Clothing Preferred: _____

_____

_____

Needed Dressing Procedure Assistance

Undergarments: _____

_____

_____

_____

_____

Slacks/Dress: _____

_____

_____

_____

_____

Shirt/Blouse: _____

_____

_____

_____

_____

Gown: _____

_____

Socks: _____

_____

_____

_____

Shoes/Slippers: _____

_____

_____

_____

_____

Belt/Suspenders: _____

_____

_____

_____

_____

Sweater: _____

_____

_____

DR. DEBI STEWART

Incontinent Care (Pads placement on bed or in chair): _____

_____

Adult Protective Garment: _____

_____

_____

Wipes/Soaps/Cleaning Help Needed: _____

_____

_____

Reminders for Toileting Needed and Frequency: _____

_____

_____

Hair Care

Assistance Needed: _____
_____

Combing/Brushing: _____
_____
_____

Styling: _____
_____
_____

Washing Instructions: _____
_____
_____
_____
_____
_____

Shampoos: _____
_____
_____

Sprays/Gels: _____
_____
_____

SECTION 7

Mobility

Ambulating

Frequency (Minimum times per day or as desired): _____

_____

Amount of Time: _____

_____

_____

Assistance Needed: _____

_____

_____

_____

Belt/Walker/Cane: _____

Amount of Usage: _____

_____

When needed: _____

_____

Other Assistance with Ambulatory Aid: _____

_____

Type of Ambulation (Limp, shuffle, normal, dragging foot): _____

_____

_____

_____

Weak Side: _____

Assistance Standing from a Sitting Position: _____

_____

_____

Lead Foot for Steps: _____

Slopes/Uneven Surfaces: _____

_____

_____

_____

Lead Foot for Entering Car: _____

Reminders Needed: _____
_____
_____
_____

Endurance (Approximate number of steps, distance, or time): _____
_____

Rising from Lying Position to Sitting Position (Include % of support needed, left—or right-side support, belts or supportive devices used):
_____
_____
_____
_____
_____
_____

Assistance Rolling to Side: _____
_____
_____
_____
_____

Assistance Lowering Feet: _____

_____

_____

_____

Assistance Rising to Sitting Position: _____

_____

_____

_____

Special Precautions: _____

_____

_____

_____

_____

Wheelchair (Pillows, pads, foam):

_____

_____

_____

Locations for Activities (Suggest using painter's tape to mark x's on floor for location for certain daily activities): _____

_____

_____

_____

_____

_____

Special Needs (Placement of utensils, plates, and glasses in reach): _____

_____

_____

_____

_____

Pathways to Keep Clear: _____

_____

_____

_____

_____

_____

_____

Lights/Switches: _____

_____

_____

_____

Towels, Toiletries: _____

_____

_____

_____

_____

Ramps: _____

_____

_____

_____

_____

Motorized Chairs (Batteries, plug-in):

_____

_____

_____

_____

_____

SECTION 8

Bedtime Routine

Dressing for Bed:

_____

_____

_____

Ambulatory Alarm: _____

_____

_____

Pajamas: _____

_____

_____

_____

Undergarments: _____

_____

_____

Door(Open/closed/partial): _____

_____

_____

_____

Lighting (Overhead, nightlight):

_____

Overhead Light: _____

_____

_____

Hall Light: _____

_____

_____

Bed Preparation: _____

_____

_____

_____

Pillows (Number and locations):

_____

_____

Pads: _____

_____

_____

_____

Sheets (Tuck/loose): _____

_____

_____

_____

Blankets (How many, how heavy):

_____

_____

**Position of Bed Rails and Foot Rails,
if Applicable:**

_____

_____

Bedside Necessities and Placement:

Eyeglasses:_____

_____

_____

Hearing Aid:_____

_____

_____

Drinking Water: _____

_____

Bell or Calling Device:_____

_____

Telephone: _____

_____

_____

**Other Household
Precautions:** _____

_____

Gates: _____

_____

Locks: _____

_____

Household Alarms: _____

_____

_____

_____

SECTION 9

Recreation/Entertainment

Where (Rocker, favorite chair, recliner): _____

_____

_____

Favorite Pastimes: Television Programs:

Program	Channel	Day of Week/Time

Games: _____
_____
_____
_____

Reading: _____
_____
_____

Crafts: _____
_____
_____

Supplies Needed/Location:
_____
_____
_____
_____

Outside the House: _____
_____
_____

Movies: _____
_____
_____
_____

Friends: _____
_____
_____

Neighbors: _____
_____
_____

Other (Computer, social networking):
_____
_____

SECTION 10

Church/Community Activities

Name of Church: _____

_____

Location: _____

_____

_____

Name of Pastor: _____

_____

Days of Meetings: _____

_____

Time of Meetings: _____

Worship Day of Week: _____

_____

Time of Worship Service: _____

_____

Preferred Seating Location: _____

_____

_____

Community Organizations: _____

_____

_____

Location: _____

_____

_____

Days of Meetings: _____

_____

_____

Time of Meetings: _____

_____

_____

SECTION 11

Restaurants/Fast Food/Eating Out

Name: _____

Location: _____

_____

Favorite Menu Item: _____

Special Instructions: _____

_____

Name: _____

Location: _____

_____

Favorite Menu Item: _____

Special Instructions: _____

_____

Name: _____

Location: _____

_____

_____

Favorite Menu Item: _____

Special Instructions: _____

_____

Name: _____
Location: _____

_____

Favorite Menu Item: _____

Special Instructions: _____

_____

Name: _____
Location: _____

_____

Favorite Menu Item: _____

Special Instructions: _____

_____

Name: _____
Location: _____

_____

_____

Favorite Menu Item: _____

_____

Special Instructions: _____

_____

Name: _____
Location: _____

_____

Favorite Menu Item: _____

_____

Special Instructions: _____

_____

Name: _____
Location: _____

_____

Favorite Menu Item: _____

_____

Special Instructions: _____

_____

SECTION 12

Special Equipment or Devices

S OME COMMON TYPES of equipment are presented in this section. It is impossible for this manual to cover all aspects of the equipment usage; therefore, a few prompts are provided and individual information should be added. This section should be reviewed by a professional (doctor, nurse, therapists) to verify accuracy of documentation.

Breathing Machines:

Continuous Positive Airway Pressure (CPAP) and Automatic Positive Airway Pressure (APAP) (location of machine, filter changing, settings, humidity)

_____

_____

_____

_____

_____

Respiratory Nebulizer Therapy Machine Procedure (Location, medication dosage added to cup, tubing, mask or mouthpiece, cleaning):

_____

_____

_____

_____

_____

When treatment given:

_____

_____

_____

Suction Machines (Settings, sterile procedure for suction catheters, cleaning canister):

_____

_____

_____

_____

Braces (Which limb or body part is supported, procedure for applying brace, where brace is stored when sleeping):

_____

_____

_____

_____

_____

Stomach tube (Inflation of bulb, checking for placement, irrigation, type of formula, dilution, gravity or pump):

_____

_____

_____

_____

PIC Line (Medication administered through line, dosage and frequency, irrigation, care of insertion site):

_____

_____

_____

_____

Traction (Attachment of weights, framework for weights, amount of weight, care of insertion points on halo traction):

_____

_____

_____

_____

Ambulation Belt: _____

_____

_____

_____

Glucose Testing (Procedure for calibrating, finger stick, reading, cleaning, and recording):

_____

_____

_____

_____

_____

Insulin Pump (Settings, refilling, attaching pump to clothing, cleaning pump): _____

_____

_____

_____

Epinephrine Pen (Epi Pen) (Location, allergy usage, administration): _____

_____

_____

_____

_____

Oxygen (Tank reading, transporting, calling for refills, mask, nasal cannula, setting number of liters percent): _____

_____

_____

_____

_____

AED Device (Location, applying pads, battery check): _____

_____

_____

_____

_____

Pulse Oximetry (Which finger(s), frequency of reading, average "normal reading"): _____

_____

_____

_____

Air Mattress (Settings, cleaning): _____

_____

_____

Intermittent Pneumonic Compression Device (IPCD) PAS (air pump compression stockings) Prevention of peripheral blood clotting in legs

SECTION 13

Communication and Sensory Impairment

Special devices (hearing aid, Braille pad, computer/typing device, voice box)

Location and instructions:

Add Pictures to Assist
with Communication

Add Pictures to Assist with Communication

SECTION 14

Brief Biography

Birthdate: _____

Childhood City/State: _____

_____

Birth Order: _____

Education: _____

_____

Military Service _____
Awards _____

_____

Dates _____
Rank _____
Active Duty _____
Job Description _____

_____

Career: _____

_____

_____

Accomplishments:

_____

_____

_____

Most Recent Employer:

_____

Job Description:

_____

_____

_____

Retirement Date: _____

_____

Other: _____

_____

Marriage Date: _____

Favorite Vacations: _____

_____

_____

Important Talents/Hobbies/Skills:

_____

Personality Traits: _____

_____

_____

Favorite Sayings: _____

_____

_____

_____

SECTION 15

Appendix

Examples

Medication

Medication/Purpose	Dosage	Frequency	Time	Special Instructions
Children's Aspirin/ Prevent blood clotting	81mg	Once daily	6:00 a.m.	Crush and mix with tsp. apple sauce

Activities

Time	Activity
6:00 a.m.	Give medications Take to bathroom, do oral care, sit in chair in kitchen for breakfast

Breakfast

Food Preferences	Special Instructions for Preparation or Serving
Scrambled egg sandwich	Toasted whole wheat bread; two eggs scrambled lightly, small amount of yellow mustard over eggs

Special Instructions

Where Eats Meals: *Kitchen table at end with wheelchair pulled up to table*

Feeding Instructions if Applicable:
Small bites, food soft, sip of liquid after every bite, ask if ready for next bite; chokes easily

Checklist for Special Procedures

- _____

- _____

- _____

- _____

- _____

- _____

- _____

- _____

Checklist for Special Procedures

- _____

- _____

- _____

- _____

- _____

- _____

- _____

- _____

Checklist for Special Procedures

- _____

- _____

- _____

- _____

- _____

- _____

- _____

- _____

Pictures

Pictures

Pictures

DR. DEBI STEWART

Updates and Notations

I. _____
_____
_____
_____
_____
_____

II. _____
_____
_____
_____
_____

III. _____
_____
_____
_____
_____

IV. _____
_____
_____

V.

_____

VI.

_____

VII.

_____

Blank Page for Notations

Blank Page for Notations

Blank Page for Notations

Blank Page for Notations

www.ingramcontent.com/pod-product-compliance
Lightning Source LLC
Chambersburg PA
CBHW031258280526
45784CB00004B/1902